□ VOYAGES OF DISCOVERY □

Storm-tossed seas were a constant threat to the early explorers. Waves could rise to a height of more than 60 feet and engulf their small ships.

TALES OF COURAGE

☐

VOYAGES OF DISCOVERY

☐

BY BRIAN WILLIAMS

Illustrated by Andrew Howat

☐

STECK-VAUGHN
L I B R A R Y
A Division of Steck-Vaughn Company
Austin, Texas

Published in the United States in 1990
by Steck-Vaughn Co., Austin, Texas,
a subsidiary of National Education Corporation.

A Cherrytree Book

Designed and produced by
A S Publishing

Library of Congress Cataloging-in-Publication Data

Williams, Brian.
    Voyages of discovery / by Brian Williams ; illustrated by Andrew
Howat
        p.   cm — (Tales of courage)
    Summary: Discusses famous sea voyages and discoveries made by
courageous voyagers.
    ISBN 0-8114-2756-0
    1. Discoveries (in geography)—Juvenile literature.
Discoveries (in geography) 2. Voyages and travel. I. Howatt,
Andrew, ill. II. Title. III. Series.
G175.W56   1990
910'.9—dc20   89-26337
                                                      CIP
                                                      AC

Printed in Italy by New Interlitho
Bound in the United States
1 2 3 4 5 6 7 8 9 0 IL 94 93 92 91 90

□ CONTENTS □

THE HIDDEN GLOBE

The oceans cover seven-tenths of the Earth. Ever since ancient times the sea has presented humans with a double challenge. It was a barrier to be overcome. Its vast expanses were daunting, unpredictable, and threatening. What unknown perils did they conceal? Yet the sea was also a pathway, a means to explore new lands. What prospects lay beyond it?

The first ocean explorers set sail thousands of years ago. Their crafts were probably made of reeds lashed together, and were propelled by oars and simple sails. In such ships Egyptians explored the Mediterranean more than 5,000 years ago, and South Americans probably ventured across the Pacific. A reed boat, flimsy though it seems, is actually very seaworthy – as Thor Heyerdahl proved in 1970 when he sailed a reed boat over 3,700 miles from Africa to Barbados. That same year four men and a cat reached Australia, after drifting on a balsa wood raft for almost 8,700 miles from South America. Early voyagers – either by accident or impelled by curiosity – must also have made voyages of such staggering distances.

Today, with fast and easy communications, it is hard to imagine a world in which so much was unknown. To sail out of sight of land was to risk being lost forever. The early sailors had no charts to guide them, no compasses to steer by, and little knowledge of winds and currents. Once at sea, they were alone.

Many of the navigators who went voyaging in search of the unknown simply vanished. Families and friends never knew what became of them. Those who returned are remembered as the great pioneers of ocean exploration: Leif Ericsson the Norseman, Cheng Ho of China, Ibn Majid the Arab, the Portuguese Magellan, the Genoese Columbus, the Englishman Cook. Each added a bit more information to the maps of the world, which were at first such a confusion of inaccurate shapes and spaces. Those whose names we know owed much to the unknown navigators who went before them, noting landmarks such as islands, headlands, and inlets and drawing simple maps to guide others.

Trade routes

It was not curiosity alone that made Europeans brave the seas. The lands of the Orient were rich in highly prized spices, beautiful silks, and other goods that merchants could sell for a profit. Carrying them home overland was hazardous and expensive. By the 1400s European merchants were anxious to find new trade routes to the East. Overland routes were closed by the expansion of the hostile Mongols and Turks who had conquered much of Asia. To find a sea route to the "Indies" – China, Indonesia, India – meant leaving the familiar coastal waters of Europe and the Mediterranean and exploring the vast empty ocean.

This urge for new trade routes sent the Portuguese south around Africa in the late 1400s, and Columbus westward across the Atlantic. Navigators sailed into Arctic waters, seeking Northeast

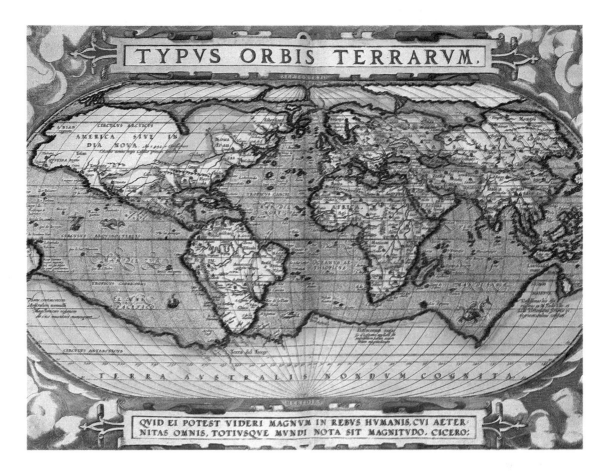

A Dutch map of the world dated 1598. The blanks were slowly being filled.

and Northwest Passages to Asia. The voyagers had no idea how large the oceans were. Columbus knew that the sun rose earlier in Genoa than in Madeira, home of his brother-in-law; therefore the Earth was round. Sailing west from Europe he was sure he would sight land eventually. He did not know how great a distance lay before him. His calculations were based on totally inaccurate world maps drawn by the Greek geographer Ptolemy a thousand years earlier.

Before 1500 the seagoing peoples of the world had little knowledge of one another's discoveries. Around the year 1000 the Vikings had explored Greenland and touched upon North America. Later the Portuguese landed on the islands of Madeira and the Azores in the Atlantic, and began to explore West Africa. The Arabs traded from the Red Sea across the northern Indian Ocean. Though expert mariners the Chinese and Japanese kept to their own waters. Europeans did not know the Pacific Ocean existed – an ocean covering a third of the world and bigger than all the land put together. Only Polynesians and South Americans had sailed the Pacific's eastern and southern expanses.

7

Life at sea

The navigators who first put our world on the map were brave and enduring almost beyond our imagining. Their ships were small, leaky, and difficult to sail. Their food was usually awful when fresh, indescribable when bad. The sailors suffered terribly from diseases such as fever, scurvy, and dysentery. They lived in cramped, unsanitary conditions for months at a stretch. Once they had left port, they disappeared into the vastness of the ocean. There was no way of sending a message back once a ship had left the regular shipping lanes – and there were few of those.

Imagine that you had to spend three years in a creaking, leaking vessel not much bigger than a modern bus. You would be frozen by polar blizzards or blistered by tropical heat; you would have to eat flour crawling with weevils and drink slimy, stagnant water. You would have no idea of where you were, whether you would ever sight land, what you would find there if you did, and how you would ever find your way home again if you survived.

Finding the way

All the exploration of the oceans, and the discovery of America, Australia, and

met their deaths in fights with local people – senseless tragedies after all they had endured and achieved. Those who returned home, including Columbus himself, often found scorn and disbelief their only reward.

In the present age of space exploration, we can compare the magnitude of the navigators' daring with a journey to Mars. A Mars mission would take three years – the same time as the ocean voyages of Magellan and Cook. The difference is that our space travelers would be in constant contact with Earth, their movements controlled by fail-safe computers and their every breath monitored. Every second would be planned, every hazard predicted. Even so, the astronauts would be on their own for the journey, a daunting prospect for which they would be thoroughly trained.

The seamen on their voyages of discovery had no training and no back-up support systems. They were alone, and usually ill-prepared. Governments were seldom interested in them until they brought back gold. An explorer was lucky to be given a first-rate ship; many set sail in vessels hastily fitted out and rotting at the seams. Captains led by example and will power. Steering into the unknown, they explored a world that turned out to be larger than anyone had previously thought. On the old maps unexplored areas were left blank and simply labeled "Here be monsters." A few explorers, brave enough to tackle the monsters, sailed into those blank spaces.

Antarctica was done in sailing ships. Those who sailed them all faced the same dangers. Across uncharted seas they were guided by the sun and stars, by simple navigational aids such as the backstaff, and by their "sea-senses" – watching waves and currents change, spotting birds in flight, or a floating branch. Not even the magnetic compass was a true ally, for it could mislead.

Wandering the oceans, many navigators failed to find land. The Vivaldis of Genoa set out westward into the Atlantic shortly before Columbus, and were never heard of again. Magellan and Cook, perhaps the greatest seamen of all,

BY WIND AND OARS

Over 2,000 years ago, a few intrepid sailors steered their ships into the gray, cold oceans of northern Europe and the Atlantic.

▫ TO THULE AND BEYOND ▫

Around 300 B.C. a small galley might have been seen moving slowly through the cold mists of the northern ocean. Its captain was Pytheas of Massalia (modern Marseilles, France). He had sailed from the warm blue Mediterranean as far north as Great Britain, exploring the coast of that unknown island, shrouded in cloud and thick green forests.

His men grumbled. They were cold and hungry, and longed for the sunshine of home. No riches were to be found in these dreary northern lands, with their savage people and bleak climate. Why go on? Last night they had been startled by the sight of a floating ice mountain, moving through the gray sea. Any farther, and they would end up in the dreaded Stagnant Sea of the North, from which no vessel could escape.

Pytheas refused to turn back. After six days, the lookout's shouts roused everyone from their misery. Land! The men peered expectantly, but saw only snow-covered mountains rising above sheer-sided inlets of cold sea. Pytheas, too, was now weary and chilled to the bone. He had had enough of wild northern lands, with their dirty, savage peoples. After landing in a small cove to refill the galley's water jars, he turned southward.

He called the land Thule – the northernmost inhabited land. It was probably Norway – less likely, Iceland. To the Greeks it represented the end of the known world. For Pytheas and his men, it held no promise; they were thankful to be heading home.

▫ THE BRENDAN VOYAGE ▫

A tiny, leather boat, without a nail in its construction, bobbed on the huge Atlan-

tic waves. Inside, sheltered from the drenching spray by oxhides, crouched its crew singing hymns. They pulled stoutly on the oars. They were crossing the second largest ocean in the world toward a land they could not be sure was there.

The rowers were risking their lives to spread the Christian Gospel. They were monks from Ireland who crossed the sea in small curraghs — tiny boats similar to those still built by the Arran islanders of the west coast of Ireland. The monks were used to making long voyages, but a monk named Brendan made the most astonishing voyage of all.

Brendan was born about A.D. 489. According to the account of his life, he set out to seek a promised land beyond the setting sun. He built a boat with a wooden frame, covered over with tightly stretched oxhide. In this, he and his companions rowed and rowed. Eventually they landed on the coast of a warm and green country, where wild grapes grew. After resting, the monks sailed home, aided by eastward-flowing currents.

The Irish monks trusted to God and their sturdy leather curragh.

Brendan was welcomed with joy by his fellow monks, and shortly afterward he died.

Could Brendan possibly have voyaged to the "Wineland" later described by Viking voyagers – to America? In 1977 historian Tim Severin tested the theory. He built a replica of Brendan's boat, using medieval materials and methods. The boat had a keel of oak, with ash wood frames lashed together with leather thongs. The frame was covered with 57 oxhides tanned with oak bark and dressed with raw wool grease. Flax thread – 23 miles of it – was used to stitch together the oxhides and make rigging for the linen sail.

The modern Brendan voyagers added a few twentieth-century refinements, such as buoyancy blocks made from polyurethane, and a life raft. They also had a radio powered by solar batteries. Otherwise, they tried to re-enact the medieval voyage as faithfully as possible.

Few people believed such a fragile-looking craft could survive in the North Atlantic. Yet Tim Severin's crew found their oxhide boat remarkably seaworthy, capable of riding the largest Atlantic waves. Even so, they needed all their endurance and determination to complete the voyage. And they knew (unlike Saint Brendan) that help was only a radio SOS away.

□ LEIF THE LUCKY □

After St. Brendan the Navigator, no European ventured far into the Atlantic for over 400 years. From around A.D. 800 the Vikings were the boldest sea-rovers of the northern seas.

Leaving their homes in Scandinavia, Vikings sailed north beyond the Arctic Circle, south around the shores of Spain into the Mediterranean, and east along the great European rivers as far as Russia and the Caspian Sea. Feared as fierce pirates and raiders, they were also traders and merchants. Above all, they were superb seamen.

A voyage to the New World

Viking ships were strong, but small. Could wooden ships of only 20 tons, less than 250 feet long and 16 feet wide, survive an Atlantic voyage in the northern latitudes?

In the year 1002 a Viking named Leif Ericsson led a voyage into the unknown. Beyond Greenland lay a new land, so it was said. He was determined to find it. Ericsson and his men were blown across an ice-cold ocean by drenching gales, their clothes soaked with spray and rain. Icicles hung from their hair and beards. Ice, snow, and fog were old foes. Even a gale was an enemy they could grapple with. Like the whales that swam in the thousands, they rode with the waves.

As the little ship crested yet another foaming wave, the sailors thanked the gods for the strength of its groaning oak timbers. After all, this was no ordinary ocean-going *hafskip*. It had swum this "whale road" before. They trusted their captain, standing in the stern beside the helmsman at the steering oar. Was he not "Leif the Lucky"? He would bring them to a safe landing, to warm fires, hot food, and horns of ale.

Some 15 years earlier this same ship, under the command of Bjarni Herjolfson, had been blown off course while on a voyage from Iceland to Greenland. With neither chart nor compass to guide

him, Herjolfson had missed southern Greenland's mountainous, treeless shore. Instead he had sighted a low-lying forested land. Herjolfson's crew did not know it but they were looking at another continent: North America.

The New World named

Some of the men who sailed with Bjarni Herjolfson were with Leif Ericsson now. They helped guide Leif to America, and made the first Viking landing at a place they called Helluland, probably Baffin Island. Hugging the coast, they sailed south, to a forested region they named Woodland (modern Labrador). Finally, they wintered in a fertile, grassy country they called Vinland – meaning either a place abundant in berries, or, more likely, rich in pasture for animals.

After barren Greenland, Vinland (modern Newfoundland) seemed an ideal place for settlement. Winter over, Leif led his men home, with tales to tell

In ships like these the Vikings made their long ocean voyages. The tent shelters and shields were protection against bad weather.

of a land to the west that was rich in timber and furs.

Leif's brother-in-law Thorfinn Karlsefni led the first group of men and women to Vinland. The small colony survived three winters. They traded with the Indians who were already living in America, but also quarreled among themselves. The Indians became hostile, and in the end the Vikings turned their backs on America.

For another 400 years America was simply forgotten. A map of the 1430s shows Vinland and mentions the names of Bjarni Herjolfson and Leif Ericsson, but these faint clues must have escaped any Europeans who saw it. The next generation of great navigators went to sea looking not for land to settle, but for new trade routes to Asia.

MASTERING THE OCEAN

Early navigators relied on the sun and stars for guidance: storms, clouds, and fogs put them in great peril. Their ships were small, leaky, and difficult to sail into the wind. Invention and courage overcame these problems.

Portugal's Prince Henry the Navigator (1394-1460) made his country the seagoing hub of the Western world. He set up a "school" for navigation and exploration. He encouraged the design of more seaworthy ships called caravels and the use of the magnetic compass. Henry sent expeditions into the Atlantic and southward to explore Africa. Each new voyage went beyond the one before.

PORTUGUESE ADVENTURES

Those first expeditions were quite literally into the unknown. Each headland seemed an obstacle. What lay beyond? The sailors had heard tales of whirlpools, sea monsters, and desert coasts strewn with bleached bones of dead men. Each day that passed was a day farther from home. In 1434 Gil Eanes was the first Portuguese captain to round Cape Bogador (now in Western Sahara). The high cliff against which the Atlantic waves beat furiously seemed a "point of no return." No one had dared venture beyond it. Eanes boldly steered past the Cape, and found calmer seas.

By 1444 the Portuguese had reached south of the Senegal River. In 1452 Diogo de Teive, sailing in the open Atlantic, came across the Azores. By Henry's

death in 1460 the coastline of Africa was becoming clearer; the blanks were beginning to be filled in.

South to the Cape

The Portuguese were tough seamen, resourceful and obedient to their commanders. The commander was crucial; should he fail, become discouraged, or show fear, his men would lose heart and all might be lost.

The story of Bartolomeu Dias began in August 1487 when he was about 30 years of age. He left Lisbon with two caravels and a small storeship crammed with provisions. A veteran of an earlier voyage to the coast of West Africa, he had been ordered to discover a sea route to India. That meant sailing farther south than any European had ever ventured.

The caravel was small, as light as 55 tons, but it could survive heavy seas. It could even be towed or rowed in a dead calm and drew so little water that it could safely navigate shallow waters. A caravel usually had three masts rigged to carry several sails — some lateen (triangular), others square. Its sails were light and easy to handle in bad weather or when men were weakened by exhaustion and sickness. Good ships they might be, but they were pitifully small for such a voyage as Dias had before him.

Instead of hugging the coast, as previous Portuguese voyagers had done, Dias struck out into the open waters of the

Dias and his men land at Walvis Bay in Africa. Ships and crew needed rest.

South Atlantic, seeking more reliable winds. Some of the crew were fearful to be out of sight of land for so long. But others were heartened by their captain's boldness. When Dias finally turned toward Africa, he left the storeship in Walvis Bay. Nine men were left aboard; they bade a sad farewell as their companions set sail. Would they meet again?

The two caravels were driven south by gales so wild that barely a stitch of canvas could be set for 13 days. No man slept much more than an hour at a time. Everyone was soaked to the skin. Still they saw no land, and the tiny ships pitched and rolled in the turbulent seas. They were experiencing the "Roaring Forties." These gales howl around the globe at a latitude of about 40° south, unchecked by land. By now the sailors'

Voyage of Bartolomeu Dias 1487-88.

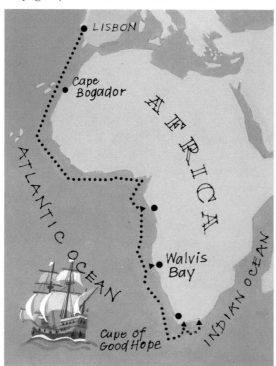

food – dried goat meat, salted fish, and coarse dry biscuits – was running low, and so was their drinking water. They were glad to catch rainwater to moisten their cracked lips: even they couldn't stomach the water in the casks, a thick, green slime alive with wriggling worms. Without fresh fruit or vegetables, the men became weakened by scurvy, the scourge of long ocean voyages.

Finally the wind eased. Dias ordered the helmsman to steer east. His outward confidence concealed a fear. Had they been blown beyond the last landfall in Africa? When the lookouts reported only empty ocean, he turned north. Might they end up sailing endlessly in circles, until the last man died?

Early in February 1488, after almost five months, they at last sighted land. They saw the southern tip of what is now South Africa. Ahead lay the Indian Ocean. They explored a little way, setting up stone pillars on shore to mark where they landed. The line of the coast was northeasterly: follow it and they must surely reach India . . .

But Dias had been at sea long enough. Weakened by disease, exhausted by the effort of sailing their tiny ships through the high seas, his men could take no more. They begged him to sail no farther. To go on was to risk mutiny. Regretfully, Dias turned for home.

The battered vessels made a slow return to Walvis Bay. They sighted the storeship 270 days after their parting. Of the nine men left on board, only three were alive. The others had died of disease – probably scurvy. They must have given up hope of ever seeing their shipmates again.

With his ships replenished – though the provisions must by now have been rot-

Only three men were still alive aboard the storeship Dias had left at Walvis Bay.

ting – Dias burned the storeship, now worm-eaten and leaking, and set course for Portugal. He reached Lisbon in December 1488. After his epic voyage, Dias received little honor. He returned to sea, as an officer under other commanders, and was drowned in 1500 in a storm off the Cape of Good Hope.

□ THE EMBASSY TO INDIA □

On July 8, 1497, four vessels, the *St. Gabriel*, the *St. Raphael*, the *Berrio*, and a storeship whose name is unknown left Portugal bound for India. The commander was a courtier-turned-navigator named Vasco da Gama.

Da Gama's orders were to go on beyond the point where Dias had turned back. The mothers, wives, and children watching from the quayside wept as the ships disappeared. Many of da Gama's men were equally miserable, the more so when the little fleet became lost in thick fog. Sails listless without wind, they drifted apart, and when the fog cleared, each ship found itself alone.

Their orders were to head for the Cape Verde Islands, and there all four vessels met up again. It was a happy reunion, and the fleet set sail in better spirits, ready to fight the gales that lay ahead.

Like Dias, da Gama chose the open ocean. But he might have changed his mind had he known it was to be 96 days before they sighted land again. More than three months seemed an eternity on the wide, empty ocean. The men's spirits sank. They feared they were sailing nowhere – that they would never see land again. Their food and water stank. They went about their daily tasks grumbling.

At last, land was sighted. The men cheered and sang with relief. Prayers were said, and the ships anchored in a sheltered bay. They were in poor condition, their hulls covered with barnacles, their sails torn and patched. The men set to work urgently on making everything shipshape.

Ahead lay unknown waters, beyond the Cape of Good Hope. On November 22, da Gama's fleet rounded the southern tip of Africa. Making slow progress against head currents and severe gales, they sailed into the Indian Ocean. They were the first Europeans to see the east coast of Africa, but few of the crew cared. Most were now sick with scurvy, and desperately weak. Men began to die, day by day. Yet still they sailed on. Relief came when they landed in Mozambique and other places where the African people were friendly. They could enjoy fresh water and fresh food, and walk on land.

The Arabs who controlled Indian Ocean trade saw the European strangers as a threat. In spite of their sufferings on the long voyage, the Portuguese were ready to use force to get their way. Da Gama bullied local rulers to make them hand over trade rights and information.

Guided across the Indian Ocean by the Arab pilot Ibn Majid, da Gama sailed into the harbor of Calicut on the west coast of India.

Arab seamen had traded across the Indian Ocean for centuries. The most experienced Arab navigator was Ibn Majid, whose seafaring feats had earned him the title "Lion of the Sea in Fury." He had written books about the Red Sea and Indian Ocean seaways. It was da Gama's great good fortune to meet Ibn Majid at Malindi. The Portuguese needed a pilot to guide them across the Indian Ocean. The third largest of the world's oceans, it was totally new to Europeans. Ibn Majid agreed to navigate the fleet to Calicut, a three-week voyage.

Everyone on board wondered what would await them in India. The Europeans knew little of the vast subcontinent, its peoples, or its ways. Portugal must have seemed very far away as the fleet sailed into the Indian port of Calicut (now Kozhikode). It was an historic moment: the first contact by sea between Europe and India.

Da Gama stayed in India three months. He made trade contacts, kept on the alert for trouble, and picked up a cargo of spices. Everyone was thankful when they set sail to return home in August 1498. But at once the winds turned

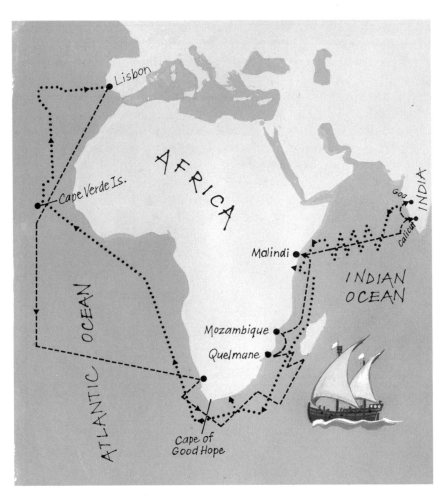

against them. It took three months to reach the African coast. So many men fell ill with scurvy that da Gama counted barely eight fit men on each of his ships. He ordered the abandonment of the *St. Raphael,* and the exhausted survivors rounded the Cape in the *St. Gabriel* and *Berrio.*

The two battered vessels became separated in a storm. The *Berrio* was first home, reaching Portugal in July 1499. Da Gama, who had stopped off in the Cape Verde Islands because his brother was dying, finally came home in September. He had been away more than two years. Not a word about the expedition had reached Portugal in his absence. For all that friends and families knew, the voyagers were dead. About two-thirds of them were.

Da Gama had given Portugal a monopoly on the spice trade and an extension of its growing empire. Although motivated primarily by a greed for India's riches, and tarnished on his second voyage (1502-03) by further acts of warlike cruelty, da Gama had earned his place in the history of European exploration. He died in India, on a third visit in 1524.

□ ADMIRAL OF THE OCEAN SEA □

Perhaps, even if they all drowned in this storm, someone, somewhere, would eventually learn of the discoveries of Christopher Columbus. Sealing an account of the voyage in a barrel, the captain hurled it into the violent sea.

For three days storms had lashed the bare-masted ship driving eastward. The helmsman struggled to keep the vessel bows-on to the sweeping seas, fearful of being caught broadside and overwhelmed. Their sister-ship had vanished. The tough Spanish seamen prayed aloud, promising to go on holy pilgrimage if their lives were spared.

On board the tiny *Niña*, Christopher Columbus was so tired that he could scarcely move a muscle. He had endured three days without sleep. He was soaked to the skin, his feet numb. He scanned the heaving horizon for a sight of land. Surely God would not allow him to perish, on the eve of his triumph?

Columbus had known danger at sea many times. He had been a sailor since he was 14, learning his seacraft in the Mediterranean. He had almost drowned in 1476, when he was 23, on his first voyage into the Atlantic. Bound for Flanders and England, his ship was sailing in convoy when it was attacked by French pirates. Seven ships went down, and nearly all Columbus's shipmates were either burned to death or drowned. He survived, clinging to an oar, and swam ashore on the coast of Portugal.

Christopher Columbus.

The road to the Indies

Lisbon, the Portuguese capital, thronged with sailors, map-makers, and dreamers. Columbus listened to their tales and studied maps. He became convinced that there must be a westerly route to the spice ports of Asia. But how long would it take? Could a ship make such a voyage?

It took Columbus years to find support for his plans. He finally found it, not in Genoa, his home port, nor in Lisbon, but at the court of the King and Queen of Spain. Not until 1492 was he ready to sail. Columbus needed tremen-

21

King Ferdinand and Queen Isabella

dous determination to overcome the doubts of the numerous people who mocked the venture. He was utterly convinced of his own mission. He had just three ships: the flagship, the *Santa Maria*, and the *Niña* and *Pinta*, which were smaller but sailed better. We have no pictures to show what they looked like.

Life for the crews on board ship was hard. The sailors slept where they could, often on the open deck. Forty men were crammed into the *Santa Maria*, only 78 feet long. The ships leaked, though the men worked at the pumps continually. Sanitation was nonexistent and the bilges stank, awash with filth.

The *Pinta* damaged its rudder before reaching the Canary Islands and the ex-pedition had to put in for repairs. Then Columbus gave the fateful order: to steer due west, into the sunset.

The sea of weeds

For two weeks the voyage went well; blown by the scudding trade winds, the ships cruised westward. But already some men were anxious. Where were the islands that geographers said abounded in the ocean? They saw just empty sea, with an occasional seabird overhead, but not a sign of land.

On "Sargasso Sunday" they were alarmed to find themselves surrounded by vast expanses of floating seaweed. For several days, this sea of weeds encompassed them.

"We shall be caught up, like sardines in a net" muttered the more fearful seamen. But Columbus laughed at their fears and pointed out that it was only "sea-grass," alive with tiny sea creatures. The ships were unhindered, and in time they left the weeds behind.

The compass lies

Columbus deliberately underestimated their daily sailing distance, to make the journey seem shorter, but he too was getting anxious. By his calculations, they should have sighted land.

Doggedly he held to his course, westward, promising a pension for the first man to sight land. A distant cloud raised false hopes, and disappointment turned to discontent. Columbus insisted they go on for at least another three days; the wind freshened, and the ships were buffeted by the biggest seas they had yet faced. But there were encouraging signs: floating vegetation borne by the current.

They had been at sea 36 days when the cry came. At 2:00 in the morning on Friday, October 12, 1492, Rodrigo de Triana was the first to sight land, though he never received the promised reward. In the darkness a white beach and a black outline of low hills was all they could make out of what seemed to be an island. They hove to and waited impatiently for daybreak.

Columbus named the island San Salvador (today Watling Island, in the Bahamas). It was small, and inhabited by curious but friendly Indians who came to the beach to watch the Spaniards row ashore. The Indians gazed wonderingly at the strangers' beards, and at the strange "tortoise shells" of bright steel (breastplates of armor) on their chests.

Unaware that he had landed in the Western Hemisphere, Columbus set sail again in search of the mainland of Asia;

The Spanish rulers agreed to fund Columbus's voyages to the Indies.

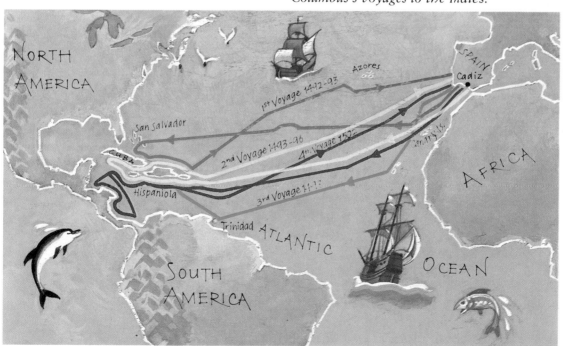

he hoped to land in Japan or China. He found many islands but little sign of gold or spices. The Spaniards were relieved at least to find no men with animal heads or similar monstrosities.

The loss of the flagship

Captain Pinzon in the *Pinta* went off exploring on his own, while Columbus sailed the coast of the large island of Hispaniola (now divided between Haiti and the Dominican Republic). To take advantage of nighttime offshore breezes, Columbus continued to sail in darkness, a risk in unknown waters. On Christmas night 1492 disaster struck.

Aboard the *Santa Maria,* the men were exhausted, and one by one fell asleep. The yawning helmsman handed the tiller to the ship's boy, whose job was to turn the sand glass every hour. It was tempting fate.

At midnight the *Santa Maria* ran aground with a terrifying jolt. Men woke to find water rushing in through smashed timbers. Lanterns flickered as they struggled to get the pumps into action. They threw spars and ballast overboard to lighten the ship. But in spite of every effort, the *Santa Maria* settled deeper onto the rock, filling rapidly. She was doomed.

Columbus gave the order to abandon ship and the crew rowed to the *Nina,* which was safe in deep water. At first light, they began salvaging whatever they could from the wreck, helped by Indians in canoes. There was enough timber to build a hut, surrounded by a stockade. With only one ship, 40 men would have to stay on the island. Columbus promised to come back to rescue them.

Now aboard the *Niña,* Columbus was relieved when the missing *Pinta* came into view. It was time to set course homeward. The two ships survived a terrible Atlantic storm on their homeward voyage, during which Columbus threw the barrel, with the scribbled account of the voyage, into the sea. The storm relented, and he reached Spain safely in March 1493.

Columbus returns to America

Within six months, Columbus was bound for the New World once more, this time with a fleet of 17 ships. He kept his promise by returning to Hispaniola, but all the castaway Spaniards were dead — either from disease or because of fights with the natives. Columbus founded a colony on the island, but became so ill himself that he almost died.

He made two more voyages to America. On the last (1502-04), he and 100 men had to abandon their worm-ridden, leaking ships and were marooned on the coast of Central America for almost a year before being rescued.

Worn out and ill, Columbus returned to Spain and died in 1506 at the age of 52. He had failed to find his new route to the East, and died unaware of the magnitude of his discovery. Only a handful of friends attended the funeral of the "Admiral of the Ocean Sea." Columbus did not even name the continent he had found. That honor went to another, Amerigo Vespucci, after whom it was named "America."

In 1500 Columbus was arrested and stripped of his command because he aroused discontent in the colony at Hispaniola. He was sent back to Spain in chains, but allowed one last voyage to the New World in 1502.

◻ FIRST AROUND THE WORLD ◻

Until the 1500s no one had ever sailed around the world. When Ferdinand Magellan led his ships west, beyond the southern tip of South America, he was heading into a new and unknown ocean – the Pacific. Not even he imagined how vast it was.

Geographers and mariners slowly realized Columbus's New World was not Asia, but a vast unknown continent. They dreamed of finding a channel leading to the sea beyond, a short cut to the Orient. A Portuguese sea captain, Ferdinand Magellan, was convinced there must be such a seaway, not northward, toward the Arctic, but south. Portugal had no interest in American adventures, so, like Columbus, Magellan turned to Spain.

Magellan in the "sea of graves." Here, off South America, his ships met high seas, howling gales, and bitter cold.

At the age of 40 he finally got his chance. With five ships and 277 men provided by the Spanish, Magellan set sail on September 20, 1519.

Magellan's route took him first west across the Atlantic, then south to Brazil to restock with fresh food and water. Beating south along the coast of South America, they discovered an inlet. Could this be the passage they sought? No, the water was fresh and grew shallow; it was the estuary of the Plate River.

Now in waters no European had ever explored, Magellan led the flotilla through what sailors later named "the sea of graves." It became bitingly cold, so cold that ice coated the rigging. It was impossible to keep clothes dry, and because of the howling blizzards the men could not light the galley fires to cook hot food.

Winter in Patagonia
On this forbidding coast, they found unfamiliar animals: black and white "goslings" (penguins), and "sea wolves" (fur seals). Magellan decided to winter ashore. His Spanish officers already questioned his authority. Discontent flared into an attempt at mutiny. Discipline was restored only after one man was hanged and another marooned.

There was fresh food, however. The sailors shot guanacos (llamalike animals), and collected shellfish. They beached the ships to scrape the barnacle-encrusted hulls and recaulk gaping seams with pitch. Magellan was determined to go on. He told his captains: "We search for the passage . . . until we find it."

The small *Santiago* (only 80 tons and with a crew of 30) went ahead of the main fleet. It was wrecked, in waves larger than any man had seen. But Magellan rescued its crew from the shore. He ordered his flag ship, the *Trinidad*, and the *Victoria* to stand away from the rocks. The *San Antonio* and *Concepcion*, however, were already too close. Magellan and his men watched in dismay as the ships were swept inshore. In the drenching rain and foaming breakers, they vanished from sight.

The watchers gave up their comrades for dead. Magellan gave the order to steer west. They rounded a point and rejoiced to see a channel leading westward. Greater still was their joy when two ships came into view; they were the missing *San Antonio* and *Concepcion*, with all banners streaming in the wind. They had escaped the rocks. And the passage was found!

Into the Pacific

This channel was no river mouth. The water had a salty sea-taste. There must be an ocean ahead. Having discovered the "Sea of the South," some of Magellan's crew had now had enough of adventuring. They wanted to turn back, but Magellan was resolute; even if they had to chew the leather off the rigging, he swore, they would sail on.

The ships put into land before venturing into the ocean. They found a desolate region. The local Indians were almost naked, despite the harsh climate, and seemed thankful for gifts of raw meat. Seeing the land by night dotted with Indian campfires, Magellan named this place Tierra del Fuego, meaning "land of fires." They were sailing between mainland South America and this large island right at its southern tip, through the channel or strait that today bears Magellan's name. There were few safe anchorages, and the pilots rowing ahead in a small boat were almost capsized by the fierce, eddying currents and whirlpools.

The voyage now seemed so dangerous that the *San Antonio*, largest of the caravels at 130 tons, deserted and sailed for home, its captain fearful of going on. The three remaining vessels restocked with fresh food, salting barrels of fish, birds, meat of seal, guanaco, and cavy (a kind of guinea pig). They ignored the green vegetables that might have saved many lives by preventing scurvy.

Eventually, the water stopped churning and lashing at the ships. They had sailed into a new ocean. It was calm and tranquil. The ship's companies held a service of thanksgiving. Cannon were fired and Magellan named the ocean "Pacific," or peaceful, because it seemed so gentle.

The days of endurance

The Pacific did indeed prove gentle for some days. Moving first north, close to the coast of Chile, then west into the huge ocean, they entered warm seas, and were delighted by "sea swallows" (flying fish) and other fish good to eat. The men were almost bored as calm day followed calm day. Magellan was disappointed not to sight land. In fact, they were heading into one of the least-islanded stretches of the Pacific. They had no idea how vast an ocean they were upon – twice the size of the Atlantic.

In the heat, their food now began to rot. The meat crawled with maggots, which chewed the ship's timber and leatherwork as well as the men's clothes. Drinking water turned yellow. Men became too weak to move. They were suf-

28

fering from scurvy, a disease that sailors recognized but knew no cure for. The effects were painful. Some men became as thin as skeletons. Others were bloated. Teeth loosened in swollen gums, and vivid swellings erupted on their skins.

For two months they glided like ghost-ships across an empty ocean. Finally, on January 25 they sighted land, a small island (possibly one of the Tuamotus). They named it after St. Paul. There was food – fish, seabirds, turtles' eggs – but no water until by good fortune rain fell. They spread out their sails and caught enough water to refill their casks.

The circle completed

Magellan pushed on again after three weeks. Starvation, temporarily staved off, soon returned, for once again the sweltering heat turned meat bad. Soon men were again bargaining their wages for dead rats. By March 1 they had eaten literally everything on board. Their last meal was a porridge made from scrapings of biscuit, plus any surviving maggots, mixed with sawdust chiseled from barrels that had once contained wine and honey. Magellan made sure every man took some, and ordered the ships to keep under sail day and night. It was their only hope, to sail as far as they could while they were still alive.

Magellan kept his crew going, by will-power alone, until March 7. Then his starving flotilla at last sighted land and was able to anchor, probably off Guam in the Marianas.

At once the ships were surrounded by islanders who paddled out in canoes and

Magellan's crew sight land after two months of Pacific wanderings.

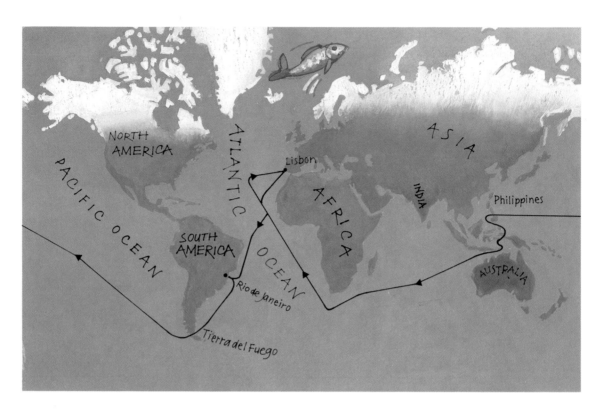

Voyage of the Magellan expedition 1519-22, the first to circle the world.

swarmed over the decks, stealing everything moveable. Many men were too weak to fight. In desperation Magellan ordered first crossbows and then cannon to be fired. The islanders fled, and the voyagers struggled ashore to steal in turn, coconuts, pigs, fruit – a feast.

Magellan treated his men well. While the sick were recovering, he visited them daily. He encouraged them to eat fresh fruit and the nourishing milk of coconuts. He was sure now that the Philippines, which he had visited in 1511, could not be far away. He sailed on westward. When an approaching canoe called out in Malay, Magellan knew he had completed the circle. He had sailed around the world in 550 days.

No hero's return

The ships anchored at the island of Mindanao, and the local ruler, the Rajah of Cebu, welcomed them. The Rajah asked to be baptized a Christian and also for help in dealing with a troublesome local chief. Magellan agreed, surely against his better judgment, and sent a raiding party to frighten the rebel into submission. The raid did not end the supposed threat, so Magellan went in person. With 60 men he found himself facing 3,000 warriors. Fighting a rear-guard action on the beach, he was killed. His Spanish officers made no move to help him, nor to retrieve his body. It seems they were glad to be rid of their Portuguese commander.

Without Magellan, there was anarchy. The *Concepcion* was scuttled, as only enough men were left to man two ships.

30

The explorers became pirates, cramming so much booty into the *Trinidad* that it began splitting apart. All Magellan's diaries and logbooks were destroyed. The men split up: half stayed on to repair the *Trinidad*, and were later hanged as pirates, while the rest departed for home under the command of Juan Sebastian del Cano.

Of the 277 men who had set out with Magellan, just 19 returned to Spain in the battered and leaking *Victoria*. They had sailed over 40,000 miles (five times farther than Columbus), mostly across unknown seas. Without Magellan to lead them, it is doubtful they would ever have crossed the Pacific, and proved once and for all that the world was truly round.

The death of Magellan in a fight with Filipino natives.

THE NORTHWEST PASSAGE

The icy seas of the Arctic are impassable for most of the year. Yet Europeans dreamed of navigating through the ice, to find new routes to Asia. Many brave men died in these bleak and freezing wastes, seeking passages that were not really there.

In 1497 John Cabot from Genoa (the same Italian city as Christopher Columbus came from) set sail from the English port of Bristol. His ship, the *Matthew*, carried only 18 men, including his son Sebastian. He sailed westward across the North Atlantic, landing either in Labrador or perhaps Cape Breton Island after 54 days at sea. Encouraged, he made a second voyage in 1498, this time with five ships. Like many voyagers Cabot believed America was actually China.

On this second voyage Cabot explored the coast of Greenland, but the cold was so bitter that his crew grew mutinous and he had to turn southward. Again he landed in what is now Canada, but found neither trade routes nor the spices and gems of the East. Historians are not sure what happened to Cabot. Only one of his five ships returned home.

◻ THE DISAPPEARANCE OF THE CORTE REALS ◻

Two Portuguese, Gaspar and Miguel Corte Real, were next to try the icy seas of the northwest. Gaspar left Lisbon in 1500, and although dismayed by the Arctic ice, he was encouraged by the sight of so many islands and bays farther west. In 1501 he returned, landed in Newfoundland and vanished. Gaspar's brother Miguel went in search of him; he too disappeared, though two of his three ships returned to Portugal safely.

◻ INTO THE ST. LAWRENCE ◻

Jacques Cartier from France arrived off the North American coast with two ships in 1534. He found a large outlet of water, flowing seaward so strongly that his ships could not sail against the current. Encouraged by this discovery, Cartier returned the following year and explored the St. Lawrence River in the ship's longboats. Beyond where Montreal now stands, impassable rapids prevented any further exploration.

◻ FOOL'S GOLD AND COLONIES ◻

Martin Frobisher sailed from England in 1576, and again in 1577 to search for the elusive Northwest Passage. When ice prevented further progress, his men took to small boats. They found some "gold" (actually worthless iron pyrites or fool's gold), and this was enough to encourage a much larger expedition in 1578 – this time to search for gold rather than a trade route. Like so many others, Frobisher returned empty-handed. Yet the

Hostile Inuits threatened Sir Martin Frobisher and his crew during their second voyage to Baffin Island in 1577.

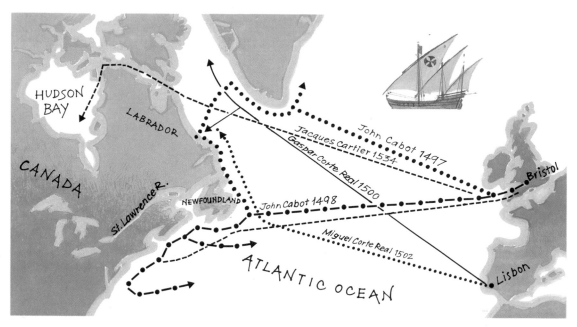

Voyages of Cabot, the Corte Reals, and Cartier.

New World was revealing riches: seas full of fish, forests of timber, and furs.

These riches tempted the first settlers to venture westward. From 1584 to 1587 the English attempted to found a colony at Roanoke Island (modern North Carolina). A relief expedition in 1590 found no trace of the brave colonists. But the courage of the navigators had opened the way. People began to leave Europe in the hope of finding new homes in a New World. In 1620 the *Mayflower* crossed the Atlantic. Its Puritan passengers hoped to find a new life free from religious persecutions at home.

□ THE DISCOVERER SET ADRIFT □

Henry Hudson, an English seaman who had sailed Arctic waters on both sides of the Atlantic, went exploring in North America in 1610. His men mutinied and Hudson, his young son, and a few comrades were cast adrift to die in an open boat. Hudson Bay, Hudson Strait, and the Hudson River are named after him.

□ THE PASSAGE MADE □

The quest for the Northwest Passage went on for centuries. In 1854 Captain Robert McClure of the *Investigator* had to abandon his ship in pack ice, but was rescued and eventually completed the passage in another vessel. Not until 1903-06 was the Northwest Passage truly conquered, by the Norwegian Roald Amundsen in his sloop *Gjoa*. Henry Larsen of the Royal Canadian Mounted Police in the *St. Roch* completed a west-east passage in 1940-42 and an east-west passage in 1944. But the Arctic waterway for which so many navigators sought in vain is too ice-bound ever to become a major shipping route.

SEARCH FOR TERRA AUSTRALIS

The Pacific Ocean is vast. European seafarers got lost there, searching for a "Great Southern Land," where they hoped to find rich kingdoms. Instead, they found a new continent, Australia, mostly desert and almost uninhabited.

The second round-the-world voyage was made by Francis Drake (1577-80). His desire was to steal trade (and gold) from the Spaniards and Portuguese rather than to increase scientific knowledge. Drake's largest vessel, the *Pelican* (later renamed the *Golden Hind*) was only 100-150 tons. It carried on board a cobbler, an apothecary, a tailor, some musicians, and a preacher, in addition to seamen, soldiers, and gentlemen. The preacher, Master Fletcher, offered prayers when the ship struck a rock in the East Indies. It was in deadly danger for 20 hours until it floated clear on the tide.

Other voyagers – the Spaniard Alvaro Mendana, the Portuguese Pedro de Quiros and Luis Vaez de Torres, the Dutchmen Isaac Le Maire and Willem Schouten – explored the mysterious South Seas. In 1605 Willem Janszoon, sailing from Batavia (modern Jakarta), came across a desert wilderness, where some crewmen were killed. This was Europe's first encounter with Australia.

The Dutch were good seamen with strong ships. They established trading posts in the East Indies. Blown by west-

Sir Francis Drake, depicted in an Elizabethan miniature.

erly gales as they rounded the Cape of Good Hope on their way to the East, some ships were wrecked on the coast of Australia, which the Dutch named New Holland. It was an unpromising land – dry and barren, inhabited only by aborigines. But how big was it, and were there any greener regions?

PILOTS OF RENOWN

Abel Tasman and his pilot Frans Visscher were ordered to find out. Their instructions were to sail to Mauritius in the Indian Ocean, turn south to pick up the Roaring Forties winds, and then see

35

where they had been blown to.

The southern ocean has the fiercest winds, the heaviest seas, and the largest icebergs in the world. The Dutch sailors in the sturdy little *Heemskirk* and *Zeehan* were constantly on watch, constantly struggling to keep their balance as the ships rolled and pitched in the seas.

After 46 days they sighted land: Tasmania. The sea around this newly discovered island proved no gentler; even today, sailors are wary of its uncertain, squally temper. Tasman pushed on and discovered New Zealand. With only primitive leadlines to sound the depth of water and with weak anchors, he had difficulty finding a safe harbor. Close to shore, sailing ships were vulnerable. Tides, currents, and winds all too often swept them helplessly onto rocks. The deep, open sea was much safer.

After a brief, and violent, encounter with New Zealand's Maoris, Tasman sailed north. He discovered the islands of Tonga and Fiji, before returning to Batavia by way of New Guinea. His had been

Dampier meets Alexander Selkirk on San Fernandez Island. Selkirk had run away to sea and joined Dampier's privateering expedition in 1703. But on the voyage he quarreled with his captain, Thomas Stradling. At his own request he was put ashore on San Fernandez, an uninhabited island. He remained there until 1709. Dampier was the pilot of the expedition that finally rescued him. Daniel Defoe based his book Robinson Crusoe *on Selkirk's adventures.*

one of the most skillful voyages of Pacific exploration.

□ BUCCANEER EXPLORER: WILLIAM DAMPIER □

The first Englishman to see Australia was William Dampier, whose life was one adventure after another. In 1683 in the *Cygnet*, he explored the Pacific, visiting Australia, but was then marooned by his mutinous crew on the Nicobar Islands. He escaped to Sumatra, became a

master-gunner in a fort, and then a buccaneer. Finally he returned to England accompanied by a tattooed Malay "wild man." Once home Dampier wrote spectacular best-sellers about his exploits.

In 1699 the British Admiralty offered Dampier command of their first official expedition to the Pacific. They gave him a single ship, the already-rotting *Roebuck*. It was so unseaworthy Dampier was forced to give up the idea of trying to sail around South America by way of stormy Cape Horn to explore Australia from the east. Instead, he voyaged around Africa, and across the Indian Ocean. Ahead lay the already known and barren western shores of "Terra Australis."

To man his leaking ship, Dampier had been given a rebellious crew and officers who disliked and envied him. He took to sleeping with loaded pistols by his side. He did manage to explore Australia's northern coast, but it was hopeless trying to sail farther.

On the return voyage, the *Roebuck* finally sank. The worm-eaten timbers had disintegrated as fast as the ship's carpenter tried to patch them. The crew took to the boats. By great good fortune, they were within rowing distance of lonely Ascension Island and eventually got back to England. Dampier's troubles were still not over. His rebellious officers had influential friends. On returning home, poor Dampier was court-martialed and stripped of all his pay.

Undaunted, he returned to sea as a trader and pirate. During his next voyage, he helped rescue Alexander Selkirk (the real life "Robinson Crusoe") from San Fernandez Island. It was Dampier's third voyage around the world. Yet he died poor and forgotten in 1715.

☐ CHARTING THE PACIFIC ☐

In the late 1700s the Pacific Ocean was still largely uncharted. The great navigator James Cook made three epic voyages that filled in much of the world map. Cook's courage and seamanship earned him an honored place in the history of exploration.

It was September 1768. The *Endeavour* heaved sluggishly as it met the first rough seas of the voyage. The ship was built not for speed but for strength. Known as a Whitby "cat," it was meant to carry coal along Britain's east coast. The ship was now headed for far distant waters.

The 400-ton three-master was a slow

Matavai Bay, Tahiti, from where Cook observed the transit of Venus. On his second voyage he returned to anchor there with his ships, Resolution *and* Adventure.

sailer, managing no more than eight knots at best. The low-railed decks were open to sea and wind. Big waves washed right over it. The storm had already swept the ship's chickens overboard, not yet a week out of Plymouth, England. The ship's cats, and a goat (which had already sailed around the world, on a previous voyage) had taken refuge below decks, seeking a dry corner.

The sailors, scrambling aloft in the rigging, were getting to know the feel of their ship. The passengers — Joseph Banks, the wealthy naturalist, and his small party of fellow botanists and artists — were seasick. Ninety-four people (the youngest aged 16, the oldest 48) and a multitude of supplies were crammed into a vessel less than 100 feet long from bow to stern. Headed south, under the command of Captain James Cook, Royal Navy, its destination was the South Seas and a place in history.

The captain's burden

Cook had much on his mind. A quiet, thoughtful Yorkshireman, he was a self-taught navigator of rare brilliance. His official mission was scientific: to visit Tahiti and there observe a transit of the planet Venus across the Sun (due on June 3, 1769, and not to recur for a century). His secret orders were to search the Pacific for unknown land, and to settle once and for all the question of whether or not a Great Southern Continent existed. If he did not find it, Cook's task was to go on looking, until he was sure it was not there.

Cook had supplies for 18 months. He had chosen the food personally, aware that sailors were often swindled by contractors who supplied horse meat instead of beef. Salt meat and biscuits were the staple diet for British seafarers. However, Cook knew the dangers of scurvy. So he had ordered barrels of "sour krout" (pickled cabbage), malt, concentrated orange and lemon juice, and a "portable soup" made from meat boiled down into solid cubes. Later he would persuade his men to eat wild celery and "scurvy grass," knowing that green vegetables helped prevent the terrible disease of scurvy.

At first the seamen refused to eat the cabbage. So Cook ordered his officers and passengers to take double helpings of the "sour krout" — and made sure the men knew about it. Convinced they must be missing out on a good thing, the crew soon began eating cabbage with relish.

Cook also saw that his ship was scrubbed clean and well aired. Foul air built up inside sealed holds; Cook had below decks "cured" with coal fires so that ventilation currents would get rid of the foul air from the bilges. He had canvas sheets rigged on deck to shield the sailors from the drenching waves in gales, and in cold weather insisted they wear the specially issued "fearnought" jackets. The men were to need warm clothing in Tierra del Fuego, at the tip of South America. Joseph Banks went ashore on its bleak coast and his two black servants froze to death there.

The Great Barrier

His scientific mission in Tahiti accomplished, Cook headed southwest to explore New Zealand. He stayed six months to make the first accurate map of North and South Island. Then he sailed west to Australia, landing at Botany Bay where Banks and his naturalists collected many new plants.

Ahead lay what the unreliable Navy charts simply called "dangerous waters." The Great Barrier Reef, the longest coral reef on Earth, stretches for 1,200 miles along Australia's eastern coast.

Cook steered his ship inside the reef to explore the coast. Not even constant depth-sounding and his seamanship could prevent disaster in such dangerous waters. The *Endeavour* grounded on the jagged coral.

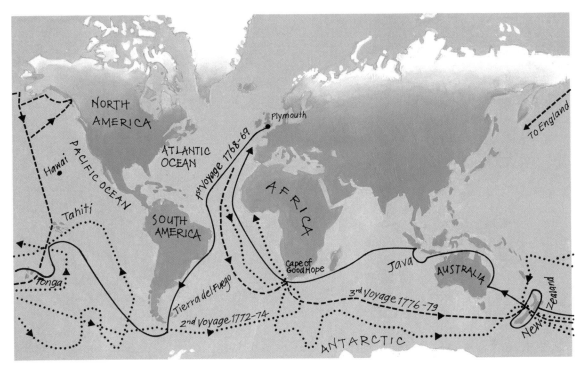

Cook's voyages 1768-79.

Cook had just gone to bed; the crunching impact brought everyone running on deck. Men scrambled aloft to take in sail, to prevent the ship moving and tearing out her hull. Down came the yards as well, until the ship was practically dismasted. Everything went over the side. The boats were lowered, and anchors taken away from the ship to a firm lodging. Using the capstan to pull on the anchor cables, they hoped to drag the *Endeavour* free. But it remained fast. Water was flooding in and relays of men worked the pumps furiously.

Cook knew he was close to losing his ship. If so, they would have to salvage as much timber as they could and somehow build another. They had no other hope of ever reaching home. No one knew where they were to rescue them.

However, the *Endeavour* repaid Cook for his faith. The flat-bottomed ship was immensely strong; even though it took in water faster than the men could pump it out, the ship finally floated. Retrieving the masts from the sea, they rerigged it and set sail as fast as possible. They had been saved by their own efforts, and by luck – a large chunk of coral was wedged into the hole in the ship's hull, partly stemming the inrush of the sea. To further staunch the flood, they tried "fothering," lashing a sail coated with tar, rags, and anything else they could find beneath the ship to cover the gash.

The *Endeavour* stayed afloat long enough for Cook to beach it for repairs. It took the crew a month of hard work. To save their precious supplies, they hunted and fished for fresh food, keeping a watch for hostile aborigines. The repairs made, they refloated the ship and sailed north to Java and then home, by way of the Cape of Good Hope. They reached England in July 1771.

Into the ocean of ice

A year later Cook was at sea again, this time in the slightly larger *Resolution*, with the *Adventure* – both Whitby coal-ships. His goal was to circle the Earth as far south as possible. They were bound for a voyage of 70,000 miles – no seamen had ever sailed so far.

Cook headed south, and in January 1773 he crossed the Antarctic Circle – the first explorer to do so. For 117 days he and his men saw no land. They met only gales, fog, and freezing cold. The Antarctic Ocean swarmed with fish and whales, yet there seemed to be no land, just endless expanses of wind-driven waves. Cook never saw the ice-sheeted mainland of the Antarctic continent, though he guessed it must be there.

Enormous icebergs glided past, gleaming in the sun. No sailing ship could penetrate the pack ice they saw ahead, and they could go no farther. Cook turned north to seek warmer seas.

After the perils of Antarctic ice, Cook's men now faced the sailors' ages-old nightmare of becoming lost in the huge, island-dotted Pacific Ocean. Once again Cook proved a master of navigation; he criss-crossed the southern Pacific until he was certain that there was no unexplored continent. He returned to the Antarctic in January 1774, reaching 71° 10′ South – a record not broken until 1823. He sailed north again to Easter Island, Tonga, New Caledonia, the South Sandwich Islands, and South Georgia. The *Resolution* returned to England in July 1775, after three years and

The death of Cook: clubbed to death in Hawaii in a dispute with the islanders.

17 days. Cook had completed an epic circumnavigation, farther south than anyone had done before. He had lost four men – one from disease, and three by drowning. Not one had died from scurvy.

The last voyage

Cook had now spent six out of seven years at sea, filling in huge blank spaces on the map of the world. He had also established friendly relations with the island peoples of the Pacific. Yet his major explorations of Australia and New Zealand attracted surprisingly little enthusiasm. Great Britain was at war with its American colonies, and saw little future in new far-distant possessions.

However, the British were still interested in finding the elusive Northwest Passage. Who better than James Cook to settle that puzzle by looking for it from the Pacific side of North America? Cook had earned a rest, but he volunteered to lead a third voyage.

In the hastily refitted *Resolution*, Cook left Plymouth in July 1776. Only a few Spaniards and Russians had explored the northwest coast of North America. This, Cook's longest and most testing voyage, would tax even his skill and courage to the utmost.

As often happened, shipyard work had been badly done. The *Resolution* had to stop at the Cape of Good Hope for repairs. The assortment of animals on board (cattle, sheep, goats, and poultry) enjoyed a few days exercise and pasture on dry land. At the Cape the *Discovery* (yet another of Cook's beloved coal-ships) joined the *Resolution*.

The voyage took them south to Tasmania and New Zealand, then northeast to Tahiti and to a new discovery – the Hawaiian islands. By early 1778 Cook was exploring the shores of what are now British Columbia in Canada, Alaska, and Siberia. Every promising inlet, however, proved a dead end. Their best hope, investigated by one of Cook's officers, William Bligh (later to command the famous *Bounty*) is now named Cook Inlet, and leads to the Alaskan city of Anchorage. They could not find the Northwest Passage, but kept on trying.

In the cold northern seas, Cook faced terrible problems with his ship's masts and rigging, which were of poor quality. Typically, he blamed himself for not checking the dockyard work. With a weary crew and worn-out ships, he at last turned south for warmer latitudes.

They made for Hawaii. Cook had always treated native people fairly. But the Hawaiians, at first friendly, became difficult. On February 13, 1779, a boat was stolen. The next day, Cook went ashore to restore order. A fight began, and the great navigator was attacked. He was viciously clubbed and stabbed to death. Like Magellan, he had died tragically in a trivial quarrel, his greatest voyage unfinished.

The *Discovery*'s captain Charles Clerke took command. He was a sick man, dying of tuberculosis that he had caught in a debtor's prison in England. He doggedly followed Cook's orders, making one more sweep north, this time toward the Kamchatka peninsula in Russia. There his strength failed. He died and was buried ashore. The expedition set sail for England, now led by Lieutenant John Gore of the *Resolution*.

News of Cook's death was sent overland. It reached London six months before the two ships. They arrived in October 1780 – having crossed the Pacific, the China and Java seas, the Indian Ocean, and the Atlantic.

No one has equaled Cook's feats. He had sailed where no European had gone before, always painstaking in his mapmaking and scientific work, always considerate toward his crew and the peoples he encountered. Somehow the names of Cook's ships – *Endeavour, Resolution, Adventure, Discovery*—seem wholly fitting memorials to the men who sailed them and the great captain who led them. A hundred years after his visit to New Zealand, the Maoris still spoke of James Cook – the "One Supreme Man in the Ship."

□ BY RAFT ACROSS THE PACIFIC □

In 1947 Thor Heyerdahl and his five companions set out to voyage from South America across the Pacific Ocean. They hoped to prove that on rafts such as theirs, sailors long ago could have made ocean voyages lasting many weeks.

Even though the enormous whale shark following them was harmless, the men on the raft kept a watchful eye out for its smaller but more ferocious cousins. Hungry sharks constantly glided beside

Thor Heyerdahl's raft Kon-Tiki *looked ramshackle, but proved strong and seaworthy.*

the *Kon-Tiki*. Norwegian scientist Thor Heyerdahl had named the raft *Kon-Tiki* after an ancient Peruvian god. He knew that a voyager-god of the Pacific islands was called Tiki. Could there be a connection? Might South Americans have voyaged across the Pacific to the distant islands? Crop plants native to South America, but growing on Polynesian islands, like sweet potatoes and cassava, were another clue. How had they got there? South American legends told of a vanished race of men, who had ruled before the Incas, but were long gone "across the sea."

The raft floats
The raft did not look like an ocean-going sailing craft. It was made from nine balsa logs cut in the forests of Ecuador and lashed together with ropes. The crew had a shelter made of bamboo canes roofed with banana leaves. Waves lapped over the half-submerged logs. "The logs will become waterlogged and you'll sink," Heyerdahl had been told before leaving Peru. But he had copied traditional South American designs: he believed the *Kon-Tiki* would float.

The outer layer of wood did become waterlogged, but the inner core wood remained dry. Nor did the ropes chafe and come apart, as had also been predicted; they merely cut into the soft wood. The ancient raft-sailors had known their business. Copying them, Heyerdahl had built a craft able to sail the Pacific. But how far?

The *Kon-Tiki* proved able to cope with rough seas. It could not be swamped; the seas simply poured over and through it, uncomfortable though this was for the crew. In bad weather,

Heyerdahl and his men lashed themselves to the raft with ropes for safety.

Flying fish and a man overboard
The voyage lasted three months. The modern-day crew found that the raft sailed surprisingly well. They passed the days fishing and studying the ocean life. Flying fish flew directly onto the raft to provide a fresh breakfast. The sharks came so close the crew would look them straight in the eye as the sleek ocean hunters cruised past the raft.

After two months their drinking water was stale and tasted bad. By bathing regularly in the sea, resting in the shade and taking salt tablets, the crew found they could manage on a much reduced water intake. They even tried eating raw plankton, caught with a fine net; the microscopic marine life made a nutritious, if rather smelly, "ocean soup."

When crewman Herman Watzinger fell overboard in a rising sea, he was lucky to survive. He slipped trying to recapture a sleeping bag caught by the wind and was rapidly left behind as the raft scudded over the waves. Swimming as hard as he could, he could not catch up and the wind hurled back the lifebelt flung in his direction. Then Knut Haugland dived in with a lifebelt and line, and swam back toward Watzinger. The two managed to catch hold of one another and their companions hauled them in. It was a narrow escape. Luckily, the sharks had kept away.

The *Kon-Tiki* made a landfall, after an encounter with a coral reef, in the Tuamotu islands of Polynesia. Heyerdahl had proved that South American raft-sailors could have crossed vast stretches of open sea.

□ COURAGEOUS VOYAGERS □

Amundsen, Roald (1872-1928) Norwegian, first to navigate the Northwest Passage (1903-06) in the 50-ton sloop *Gjoa*. Also first to reach the South Pole in 1911.

Anson, George (1697-1762) British admiral, sailed around the world 1740-44, reformed Royal Navy, and encouraged voyages of discovery.

Baffin, William (1584-1622) English navigator who discovered Baffin Bay. No voyager sailed farther north for 236 years.

Barents, Willem (d. 1597) Dutch, perished after wintering in the Arctic seeking the Northeast Passage. Discovered Spitzbergen (1596).

over 3,700 miles to Timor in the East Indies.

Blyth, Chay (b. 1940) British, first person to sail single-handed around the world in an east-west direction (against prevailing winds) in 1970-71. In 1966 rowed the Atlantic with John Ridgway.

Bougainville, Louis Antoine de (1729-1811) French navigator of the Pacific, sailed around the world 1766-69 in *La Boudeuse*.

Brendan the Navigator (485-577) Irish saint, who (legend tells) sailed the Atlantic to the west. May have reached America.

Cabot, John (1450-98) Italian who sailed under English flag to seek the Northwest Passage

Barents's ship stranded in the Arctic ice, while his men hunt for driftwood to burn as fuel.

Bering, Vitus (1681-1741) Danish, discovered strait between Siberia and Alaska, proving that Asia and America were not joined. Died of cold and hunger on second Arctic voyage.

Bligh, William (1754-1817) British, sailed with Cook on third voyage. In 1787 commanded HMS *Bounty* on voyage to South Seas. When crew mutinied in Tahiti, Bligh and 18 others were cast adrift in an open boat, and sailed

(1497, 1498). His son Sebastian (about 1474-1557) explored Hudson Bay (1508), thinking it to be a sea leading to Asia.

Cabral, Pedro Alvares (about 1460-about 1526) Portuguese voyager who in 1500 sailed to Brazil, southern Africa, and India.

Cartier, Jacques (1491-1557) French sailor who sailed three times to Canada, and discovered the St. Lawrence River (1535).

Cheng Ho (d. 1435) Chinese admiral who led seven fleets to East Indies, Sri Lanka, and the Persian Gulf (1405-33), seeking new trade links.

Chichester, Sir Francis (1901-72) British aviator and lone sailor, made single-handed voyage around the world in 1967 at the age of 65.

Columbus, Christopher (1451-1506) Genoese, first European to sail to America since Vikings. Made four voyages, hoping to find a faster sailing route to Asia, which he believed America to be.

Cook, James (1728-79) British navigator whose three voyages settled the main remaining doubts about the geography of the Pacific and Australia, and Oceania. The last and greatest of the ocean explorers.

Corte Real, Gaspar (about 1450-1501) Portuguese navigator who sailed twice to North America, vanishing on his second voyage. His brother **Miguel** disappeared in 1502 while searching for him.

da Gama, Vasco (1469-1524) Portuguese, first European to sail to India by way of the Cape of Good Hope (1497-99).

Dampier, William (1652-1715) British buccaneer and adventurer, who explored coasts of Australia and New Guinea. Sailed around the world three times.

Davis, John (about 1550-1605) English navigator who explored shores of Greenland and Canada, and later discovered the Falkland Islands. Killed by pirates near Singapore.

Dee, John (1527-1608) English, geographer for Queen Elizabeth I, for whom he drew up accounts of the navigators' discoveries.

Dias, Bartolomeu (about 1450-1500) Portuguese captain who was the first to sail around the southern tip of Africa into the Indian Ocean (1488).

Drake, Sir Francis (1540-1596) first Englishman to sail around the world (1577-80); brought potatoes and tobacco from Virginia colony (1586), fought the Spanish Armada (1588), died in Caribbean.

Ericsson, Leif (about 1000) Norse navigator who sailed from Greenland to "Vinland" (North America). Son of Eric the Red who discovered Greenland in 982.

The largest of Cheng Ho's ships had four decks and watertight compartments.

Portrait of Vasco da Gama

Flinders, Matthew (1774-1814) British, explored coast of New South Wales, Australia (with George Bass). Also sailed around Tasmania and surveyed west coast of Australia (1801-03).

Francis, Clare (b. 1946) British lone sailor, who set a women's record for a solo voyage across the Atlantic of 29 days in 1976.

Franklin, Sir John (1786-1847) British seeker after the Northwest Passage. Died after his vessels became trapped in polar ice.

Frobisher, Sir Martin (about 1535-94) English, sailed on trading voyages to Africa, made three unsuccessful searches for the Northwest Passage in the 1570s.

Hakluyt, Richard (about 1552-1616) English geographer whose book *Principal Voyages and Discoveries of the English Nation* (1589) records the adventures of the early navigators.

Hall, Charles Francis (1812-71) American Arctic voyager, died while commanding steamer *Polaris*, some of whose crew spent six months adrift on floating ice.

Hanno (5th-6th century B.C.) Phoenician sailor who ventured out of the Mediterranean and explored the coast of Africa.

Henry the Navigator (1394-1460) Portuguese prince who sent ships out into the Atlantic and south to explore the coast of Africa.

Heyerdahl, Thor (b. 1914) Norwegian scientist-explorer, famous for his voyages in the raft *Kon-Tiki* and reed boat *Ra;* also sailed reed boat *Tigris* from Asia to Africa.

Magellan, Ferdinand (1480-1521) Portuguese, leader of first expedition to sail around the world. Killed before the voyage was completed.

McClure, Sir Robert (1807-73) British naval officer who discovered the Northwest Passage in 1854 while searching for Franklin.

Mendana de Neyra, Alvaro de (1541-95) Spaniard who sailed into the Pacific and discovered the Solomon Islands about 1567.

Nansen, Fridtjof (1861-1930) Norwegian who let his ship *Fram* drift with the Arctic ice to reach what was then (1895) the northernmost point reached.

Nordenskjold, Baron Nils (1832-1901) Swedish, first man to navigate the Northeast Passage, 1878-80, in the *Vega*.

Peary, Robert E. (1856-1920) American, with Matthew Henson and 4 Eskimos, first to reach North Pole in 1909.

Pinzon, Martin (about 1440-93) Spaniard who sailed with Columbus. In command of the *Pinta*. Died days after returning to Spain. His brother Vicente (about 1460-about 1524) commanded the *Nina* and later explored South American coast.

Ponce de Leon, Juan (about 1460-1521) Spanish, sailed on Columbus's second voyage in 1493, discovered Florida in 1513.

Pytheas (late 4th century B.C.) Greek who explored coasts of Spain, France, and Britain, and is thought to have sighted Norway.

Schouten, Willem (about 1567-1625) Dutch navigator who with Isaac Le Maire explored the East Indies and sailed around Cape Horn and back, naming the stormy Cape after his birthplace in Holland.

Slocum, Joshua (1844-1909?) Canadian, first to sail around the world alone. In his yacht *Spray* he left Boston in 1895 and returned three years later. Disappeared on a voyage to South America.

Tasman, Abel Janszoon (1603-59) Dutch navigator sent from East Indies by Governor Van Diemen to explore Australian waters. Discovered Tasmania and New Zealand, also sighted northern Australia.

Torres, Luis Vaez de (early 1600s) Spanish, sailed around New Guinea and almost discovered Australia (1615). The Torres Strait is named after him.

Vespucci, Amerigo (1454-1512) Florence-born explorer, sailed with Alonso de Ojeda in 1499 to America – which is named after him. Explored coast of South America (1501).

Ferdinand Magellan

Amerigo Vespucci

□ INDEX □